THE CHAMPION'S GUIDE TO APEX LEGENDS

Silver Dolphin Books
An imprint of Printers Row Publishing Group
A division of Readerlink Distribution Services, LLC
10350 Barnes Canyon Road, Suite 100, San Diego, CA 92121
www.silverdolphinbooks.com

Printers Row Publishing Group is a division of Readerlink Distribution Services, LLC.
Silver Dolphin Books is a registered trademark of Readerlink Distributions Services, LLC.

All notations of errors or omissions should be addressed to Silver Dolphin Books, Editorial
Department, at the above address. All other correspondence (author inquiries, permissions)
concerning the content of this book should be addressed to: info@characterarts.com

Written by Dom Peppiatt

ISBN: 978-1-64517-179-9

Manufactured, printed, and assembled in Stevens Point, Wisconsin, USA.
First printing, August 2019. WOR/08/19.
23 22 21 20 19 1 2 3 4 5

THE CHAMPION'S GUIDE TO APEX LEGENDS

EVERYTHING YOU NEED TO DOMINATE THE BATTLE ROYALE

Silver Dolphin

CONTENTS

CLASS BREAKDOWN

10 THINGS TO KNOW

WELCOME TO APEX LEGENDS, THE NEWEST HIT GAME FROM RESPAWN ENTERTAINMENT. HERE'S THE MOST VITAL INFORMATION YOU NEED TO KNOW ABOUT THE GAME.

1 WHAT IS APEX LEGENDS?

Apex Legends is a first-person, squad-based Battle Royale game with Hero Shooter elements designed for Xbox One, PC, and PlayStation 4 that anyone can play for free.

2 THE NEXT EVOLUTION OF BATTLE ROYALE

Show 'em what you're made of in Apex Legends, a free-to-play Battle Royale game where contenders from across the Frontier team up to battle for glory, fame, and fortune.

WHAT IS A BATTLE ROYALE?

Battle Royales are competitive games that pit up to 100 players against each other in a last-man-standing firefight. The map shrinks, bringing players closer to each other as time runs out.

3 WHAT MAKES APEX LEGENDS DIFFERENT?

Apex Legends introduces Legends into the genre: individual characters who have unique traits and abilities that allow them to dominate the battlefield in different ways. You are also put on a squad, battling to be the best of 60 players.

4 WHO MADE APEX LEGENDS?

Apex Legends was made by Respawn Entertainment. The developer also made *Titanfall* and *Titanfall 2*, and is currently working on a *Star Wars* game, too. The studio is known for fast, movement-focused FPS games, and was founded by ex–Call of Duty developers.

5

HOW MUCH DOES IT COST?

Apex Legends has been—and always will be—free. The game is a free-to-play title, supported by microtransactions that come in the form of Apex Coins. These coins can be exchanged for Apex Packs (which contain cosmetic items), but the base game will never cost a penny.

6

WHERE CAN I PLAY IT?

Apex Legends is available to download on the Xbox One, PlayStation 4, and PC (via Origin). You will need an Internet connection to play, since everything in this game takes place online. There is no solo offline mode.

7

WHAT MATURITY RATING IS THIS GAME?

The ESRB rates *Apex Legends* as Teen, or 13 and older, in the US, and comes with a PEGI 16 rating in the UK. The Finisher moves are the closest to real violence the game gets, but otherwise there is no blood, gore, or crude language.

8

HOW MANY CHARACTERS ARE THERE?

There are nine playable characters in *Apex Legends*: Bangalore, Bloodhound, Caustic, Gibraltar, Lifeline, Mirage, Octane, Pathfinder, and Wraith. But Respawn plans to add more characters all the time.

9

HOW DO I GET BETTER AT THE GAME?

Time, patience, and dedication! But there are many skills you can learn that will help you master the game and get the advantage over other players—hopefully this book can help you learn some of the most important tricks.

10

I'M NEW—AM I TOO LATE TO THE GAME?

Not at all! *Apex Legends* continues to grow and add new players all the time. The matchmaking system in the game connects players of all skill levels into matches even today, so there's no better time to start playing.

LEARN THE BASICS

APEX LEGENDS MAY SEEM LIKE A SIMPLE GAME, BUT THERE IS A SERIES OF RULES YOU NEED TO KNOW BEFORE YOU START PLAYING.

FOLLOWING RUSSMAUS

THE BASICS

Each *Apex Legends* game consists of up to 60 players working together in teams of three. There is a maximum of 20 teams in every game, though this may be lower, depending on the matchmaking process.

Players have 100 health, and can reduce damage taken by picking up armor or helmets. You will be knocked down if you take 100 damage to your health, and you will be killed if you take 50 damage while knocked down.

You can be revived by teammates when knocked down, and you can be respawned by teammates after being killed. If your teammates fail to revive or respawn you within the time limit, you will be eliminated. If all three members of your team are killed, your team is eliminated from the game.

You deal damage with weapons, which can be picked up from the ground, loot bins, or other players. Each weapon will need to be upgraded with attachments you can find on the map.

ROUNDS

Apex Legends **matches are split into Rounds.** You can tell which Round you're in because the announcer will say it, or you'll see it under your minimap. There is a maximum of eight rounds in each match, some of which are broken up with Wait and Closing periods. Wait shows you where the map will close to, and Closing forces you to move in.

Anyone outside the Ring will suffer Health damage every 1.5 seconds, the amount of which changes each Round. The longer the game goes on, less of the map is playable, reducing by up to 1115m per Round.

WINNING

The last team standing will win the game. It is possible to win the game when knocked down or killed, if your team makes it to the end of the game.

The winning team will receive bonus XP at the end of the game, even if one or two members have been killed. You will not receive XP if you leave the game once you're knocked down or killed.

HEADS UP

TO BE VICTORIOUS AT APEX LEGENDS, YOU HAVE TO UNDERSTAND WHAT YOU'RE LOOKING AT ON-SCREEN, AND HOW TO PLAY.

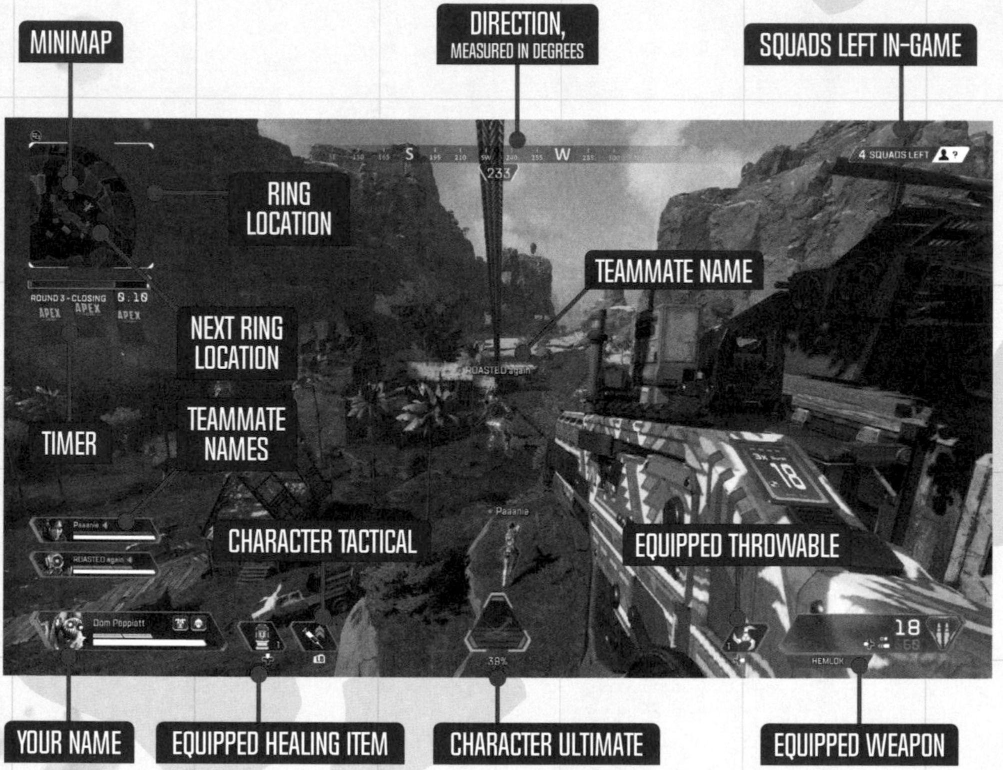

MINIMAP
DIRECTION, MEASURED IN DEGREES
SQUADS LEFT IN-GAME
4 SQUADS LEFT
233
RING LOCATION
TEAMMATE NAME
ROUND 3 - CLOSING
NEXT RING LOCATION
ROASTED again
TIMER
TEAMMATE NAMES
Paaanie
CHARACTER TACTICAL
EQUIPPED THROWABLE
Dom Peppiatt
39%
18
HEMLOK
YOUR NAME
EQUIPPED HEALING ITEM
CHARACTER ULTIMATE
EQUIPPED WEAPON

IN CONTROL

XBOX CONTROLLER

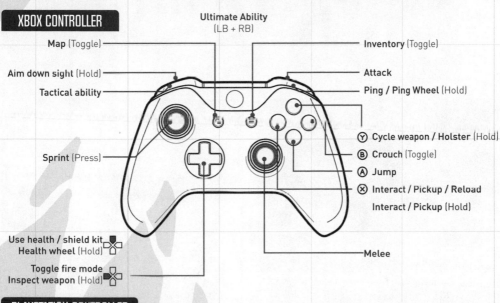

Ultimate Ability
(LB + RB)

Map (Toggle)

Aim down sight (Hold)

Tactical ability

Sprint (Press)

Inventory (Toggle)

Attack

Ping / Ping Wheel (Hold)

Ⓨ Cycle weapon / Holster (Hold)
Ⓑ Crouch (Toggle)
Ⓐ Jump
Ⓧ Interact / Pickup / Reload
Interact / Pickup (Hold)

Use health / shield kit
Health wheel (Hold)

Toggle fire mode
Inspect weapon (Hold)

Melee

PLAYSTATION CONTROLLER

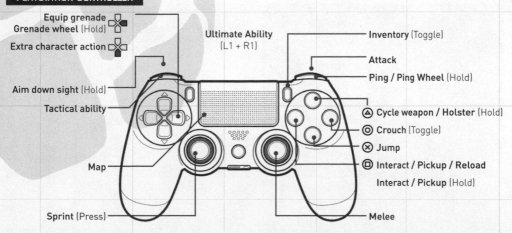

Equip grenade
Grenade wheel (Hold)

Extra character action

Aim down sight (Hold)

Tactical ability

Ultimate Ability
(L1 + R1)

Inventory (Toggle)

Attack

Ping / Ping Wheel (Hold)

△ Cycle weapon / Holster (Hold)
○ Crouch (Toggle)
✕ Jump
□ Interact / Pickup / Reload
Interact / Pickup (Hold)

Map

Sprint (Press)

Melee

•11

TERMS OF ENGAGEMENT

USE THIS GLOSSARY TO GET TO KNOW THE GAME'S KEY ELEMENTS.

DEATH BOX

The boxes enemies leave behind once they've been eliminated, full of all the loot they found.

RESPAWN BEACON

Identified with a green light, these machines will call your allies back into the map via a drop ship.

LOOT TICK

Small (but valuable!) robots that like to hide around the map. Listen for their beeping; they drop great loot!

PING

An action that notifies allies of a point of interest: an enemy, item, location, death box, or downed ally.

RING

The moving wall that determines the game area. Stay inside it, or you'll begin to take damage.

HOT ZONE

The best place to land in the early game. This area is usually hotly contested but offers great rewards.

ABILITIES

Each of the playable characters in the game has three unique abilities: a passive, a tactical, and an ultimate.

KNOCKED

The term for when you get taken down—losing your 100 health—but before you get killed. Vulnerable to finishers.

CHAMPION

The player with the most kills in the game. Take out a Champion for a bonus 500XP at the end of your game.

LOOT

The term for any item that can be picked up. Each piece of loot has a level: Common, Rare, Legendary, or Epic.

KING'S CANYON

THE GAME'S MAP IS A WILD AND VARIED LANDSCAPE. HERE'S EVERYTHING YOU NEED TO KNOW TO TAME IT.

ARTILLERY

SLUM LAKES

RELAY

THE PIT

WETLANDS

CASCADES

RUNOFF

BUNKER

SWAMPS

AIRBASE

BRIDGES

HYDRO DAM

MARKET

SKULL TOWN

REPULSOR

Apex Legends was built to be a fast, mobile game played in squads of three. It sounds obvious, but keep this in mind while exploring: always move.

THUNDERDOME

WATER TREATMENT

KEY LOCATIONS

Most guns and abilities are designed to work best at mid- or close-range—don't take potshots across the map at well-fortified enemies: you'll just give yourself away!

ARTILLERY

Though zip lines connect the three large buildings—making it a quick place to loot—Artillery is massively popular as a landing zone, meaning you usually have to fight off a few teams to take advantage of the good loot.

RELAY

Relay is positioned ideally for teams that like to raid and run, and rarely has many people dead set on exploring it. It's good for quick raids, but thanks to its mix of high and low ground, it's not a great place to stick around.

AIRBASE

If you're a daredevil, this one's for you: two massive, exposed runways (connected with a zip line) are home to good loot … but be aware that you're always likely to be in someone's sights out here.

SWAMPS

With the largest amount of loot in one place, Swamps is a great landing location for both the number of things you can find and the size of the zone. Escaping is tricky, though, thanks to where Swamps sits on the map.

KEY LOCATIONS (CONTINUED)

You can climb doors: open one, and wall-climb on top of it. This can be a handy way of surprising raiding teams or getting the jump on unsuspecting players.

THUNDERDOME

A great location for dynamic firefights between the suspended cages and rocks, this location is home to a handy Respawn Beacon and some good loot spread across the various interconnected levels.

BUNKER

An intense, awkward central corridor that often houses good loot, and almost always ends in a collision with another team. Good projectile users flourish here—just watch out for Caustic mains and ambushes behind doors.

THE PIT

Thanks to how secluded it is, The Pit looks tempting at first, but be warned: there's no cover, and enemies can get the jump on you from three entry points. Loot Ticks like it here, but so do roving enemy teams.

SKULL TOWN

This is one of the busiest drop zones thanks to its central location. A smart player aims for the rooftops here: get a gun, pick off weak players, stay indoors, and heal up. Don't stick around and get trapped.

Don't ignore the red balloons—these can redeploy you in a pinch, and can help you outrun the ring as it closes in, too. Think tactically, and these balloons can be a lifesaver.

WETLANDS

It's quick to raid the dozen-or-so buildings that make up the Wetlands. Afterwards, you can focus on pushing through the easily defended choke point to Artillery. Even non-Pathfinder players can command the rooftops here.

WATCHTOWER NORTH

With the nearest Respawn Beacon located in Cascades, you know you've got a fight on your hands if you're knocked down here. Don't worry though—a good vantage point and decent amounts of loot make for a solid area.

RUNOFF

If you land in Runoff—and live—you'll come away all geared up. Thanks to the massive amount of loot here, it's a hotspot...and there are no conveniently located Respawn Beacons. A high-risk, high-reward zone.

SLUM LAKES

A fairly popular landing zone, this knot of small buildings has a lot of loot, but you're unlikely to find much high-level gear. From here, if you need more loot, head to Runoff or The Pit.

THE JUMP

THE JUMP IS WHERE IT ALL BEGINS. IT'S WHERE LEGENDS ARE BORN. MAKE SURE YOU KNOW HOW TO GET THE FIRST STEPS OF YOUR JOURNEY RIGHT.

Apex Legends **is all about surviving for as long as possible, and that means nailing your landing and starting your game off right.** Are you a dive-bomber or a glider? Did you know that you can taper off your initial free fall into a more controlled glide once you get full control over your character? Have you ever been the victim of a jumpmaster pushing you away from your teammates on a big red balloon? (And do you want to make sure that never happens again?) Then read on to discover some essential tips behind the perfect jump.

DO
Keep an eye out for other players' contrails: these are the best visual indicators of where other players are going to land. If you see lots of colors mingling together, you might want to keep your distance.

DON'T
Assume the jump ends when you near the ground: you can maintain the momentum from your fall even when you approach King's Canyon, meaning skilled players can launch themselves even further with enough practice.

DON'T Let the jumpmaster do all the work. When you near the landing zone, make sure to split off from your boss early—stick close, but peel off. This way, you're not fighting for loot and taking each other's things.

DO Listen to your friends' suggestions: if you're playing with randoms, they may have a lot of experience in one area if they're pinging it over and over again. Have confidence in your choices, but remember to work as a team!

FOLLOWING RUSSMAUS
Hold X Stop Following

DON'T Abandon your teammates. This game is designed for three players and you'll notice *Apex Legends* is a very unforgiving experience if you hightail it to the other end of the map without your friends. Solo players don't get respawned.

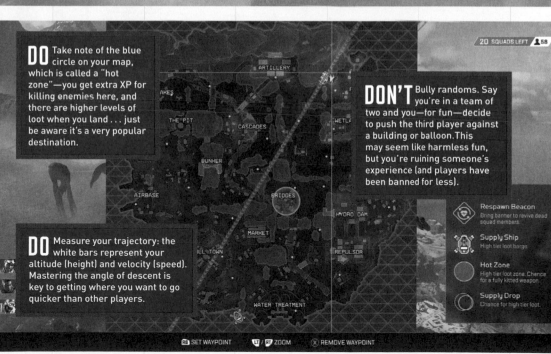

DO Take note of the blue circle on your map, which is called a "hot zone"—you get extra XP for killing enemies here, and there are higher levels of loot when you land . . . just be aware it's a very popular destination.

DON'T Bully randoms. Say you're in a team of two and you—for fun—decide to push the third player against a building or balloon. This may seem like harmless fun, but you're ruining someone's experience (and players have been banned for less).

DO Measure your trajectory: the white bars represent your altitude (height) and velocity (speed). Mastering the angle of descent is key to getting where you want to go quicker than other players.

20 SQUADS LEFT 58

ARTILLERY
AKES
THE PIT
CASCADES
WETL
BUNKER
AIRBASE
BRIDGES
HYDRO DAM
MARKET
ILL TOWN
REPULSOR
WATER TREATMENT

Respawn Beacon
Bring banner to revive dead squad members.

Supply Ship
High tier loot barge.

Hot Zone
High tier loot zone. Chance for a fully kitted weapon.

Supply Drop
Chance for high tier loot.

RB SET WAYPOINT   LT / RT ZOOM   X REMOVE WAYPOINT

BANGALORE

COCKY, CONFIDENT, AND A CRACK SHOT, BANGALORE IS THE LAST PERSON YOU WANT TO FACE ON THE BATTLEFIELD.

Bangalore—real name, Anita Williams—was born into a military family. Everyone (and everything) she knew growing up was IMC. Thanks to being raised in a ruthless, well-oiled military family, Bangalore has been proficient with just about every weapon since she was a child.

Bangalore's mastery of the weapons she uses is legendary; she can take apart a gun and put it back together in seconds. Blindfolded. She's a real pro. Three years ago, Bangalore and her brother went on a mission for the IMC, tasked with fetching a fleet of mercenaries from the Outlands in order to recruit them against the Militia.

It seems her mission was a trap, though, and she was separated from her brother. Now alone, and harboring a deadly grudge, Bangalore fights in the Apex Games in the hope of raising funds to get her back to her family.

PASSIVE — DOUBLE TIME

Taking fire when Sprint is active will increase your speed by 30% for a short amount of time. Best used to accelerate to cover, or as a speed boost for returning fire.

TACTICAL — SMOKE LAUNCHER

A high-velocity smoke canister you can detonate to create a smoke wall. Handy for escaping enemies or suppressing unsuspecting teams.

ULTIMATE — ROLLING THUNDER

An artillery strike that peppers a large area with ballistic missiles, killing any downed players—friendly or hostile. Best used for large-scale fights or ambushes.

Bangalore is a great beginner character thanks to her traditional FPS setup. Newbies should start with her.

Be careful when combating Bloodhound players as a Bangalore: his ultimate allows him to see through smoke, ruining the element of surprise.

Don't be shy about using Smoke Launcher: it has a low cooldown and lends itself to frequent, aggressive use.

BLOODHOUND

A MYSTERIOUS TRACKER WITH THE POWER OF GODS ON THEIR SIDE, BLOODHOUND IS AS FEARSOME AS THEY ARE UNPREDICTABLE.

Throughout the Outlands, people know Bloodhound as one of the greatest hunters in history. But despite their (in)famous status, people know practically nothing else about this mysterious prodigy. Some say they're a former slave out for revenge; some say they talk to the gods; some say they're a rich vigilante that happens to be half bat.

For all the hearsay, what's truly known of Bloodhound is this: they're lethal. Whispers suggest the technological tracker calls upon Earth's Norse gods for aim in times of need, but no one knows for sure. No one even knows where Bloodhound came from, or what their real name is.

Bloodhound believes in fate—that everyone who meets them has had their destiny predetermined...and that's probably true, because as soon as they know Bloodhound is near, they're as good as dead.

PASSIVE — TRACKER

Lets you see tracks left by your enemies and how recently they were active. Very useful for predicting enemy movement and locking down a whole team's position.

TACTICAL — EYE OF THE ALLFATHER

Briefly reveal hidden enemies, traps, and clues in buildings and foliage in front of you. Use this to scope out new areas.

ULTIMATE — BEAST OF THE HUNT

Activating this ability may take a little while, but it gives a boost to your speed and highlights enemies. Use this speed to bear down on your foes.

Bloodhound comes into their own in choke points: fire up your ultimate to put the pressure on and share the locations of enemy teams with your squad.

Though Bloodhound's ultimate normally takes a little while to warm up, activating it while climbing a wall readies it immediately.

Bloodhound players are big boons to the team. Make sure you ping enemy tracks located via Tracker: your teammates can't see what you see!

30　NE　40　75　E　105
59
Ring closing in:

3:26

ROUND 2

Door Used [22m]
Age 47 Sec

CLASS BREAKDOWN

CAUSTIC

A BRILLIANT, TWISTED MIND AND A MASTER OF TRAPS AND POISON ATTACKS, THIS LEGEND THRIVES ON THE ELEMENT OF SURPRISE.

Caustic's motives for entering the Apex Games are perhaps the most sinister of all the Legends. The man, once known as Alexander Nox, is a scientist with a hunger for experimentation. Once the bright young head scientist of a leading Frontier pesticide manufacturer, Nox became obsessed with how his chemicals could eat away at anything they touched.

The once-idealistic scientist worked day and night on new formulas, turning from an eager chemist into a twisted madman who experimented on living tissues.

After alarming his bosses with his unethical experiments, Nox went missing and was presumed dead. Humbert Labs burned to the ground and its employees were dead. Nox went dark, off the grid. However, a new competitor named Caustic soon started gaining notoriety in the Apex Games, eager to test lethal new chemical concoctions . . .

PASSIVE — NOX VISION

Allows you to see enemies through your gas—which is incredibly handy if you've detonated traps and thrown grenades into an enemy team's position.

TACTICAL — NOX GAS TRAP

Drop canisters that release deadly Nox gas when shot or triggered by enemies. The traps impair your opponents' vision and slow down their movement.

ULTIMATE — NOX GAS GRENADE

Blankets a large area in Nox gas: the best endgame tactical ability, as it can pollute most of the smallest game ring, affecting multiple enemies at once.

Because enemies who trigger Caustic's traps become visible on your map, Caustic is a great tool for detecting an enemy presence early.

Be mindful of your positioning when using Caustic: his abilities hurt allies. Make sure to splinter off from your squad when engaging enemy positions.

Push when you have ultimate. Caustic can be a real pain to escape from when his vision is active and you can't see or move very far.

GIBRALTAR

AS STURDY AS THE ROCK HE'S NAMED AFTER, GIBRALTAR IS, SOMETIMES LITERALLY, AN IMMOVABLE PRESENCE ON THE BATTLEFIELD.

Makoa Gibraltar, the 30-year-old gentle giant from the planet Solace, is the son of two Search and Rescue Association of Solace volunteers, and it shows in his personality. Gibraltar's main priority is getting others out of danger—something he learned the hard way when his father lost his arm saving him and his boyfriend from a mudslide.

After discovering a life of mischief wasn't for him, the big defender decided to look elsewhere for fulfillment. Gibraltar came to the Apex Games after seeing many of his friends and loved ones join the tournament in the hopes of cashing in—but getting badly hurt in the process. Now, he plays in the games with the express purpose of putting himself in the line of fire in order to protect them, putting his rebellious nature and good heart to work.

PASSIVE

GUN SHIELD

Aiming down sights deploys a gun shield that blocks incoming fire. This makes Gibraltar the best tank in the game, soaking up bullets and laying down suppressing fire.

TACTICAL

DOME-SHIELD

Deploys a dome-shield that blocks attacks, active for 15 seconds. A versatile gadget that even gives you enough time to pick up downed allies.

ULTIMATE

BOMBARDMENT

Calls in a focused mortar strike on a marked position. The second you can use this in a firefight, do so: it deals massive damage and is hard to escape.

Gibraltar's ultimate has very good range: throw the device used to call in Bombardment as far as you can and see distant teams scramble for safety!

The Dome of Protection isn't a wall—don't get blindsided by enemies sneaking around it to take you by surprise.

Gibraltar players like shotguns: the shield that pops up when aiming down sights means close-range encounters work better than long-range ones.

LIFELINE

DEDICATED, UNCOMPROMISING, AND INTELLIGENT, LIFELINE IS ALWAYS AT THE CRUX OF AN APEX TEAM THAT WORKS TOGETHER.

Of all the people battling it out in the Apex Games, Ajay Che (alias Lifeline) is perhaps the most unlikely. The selfless combat medic was appalled to learn that her parents were incredibly wealthy war profiteers, and moved away as soon as she discovered the horrors they helped enable.

She soon enlisted in the Frontier Corps: a humanitarian outfit that prides itself on helping out communities in peril. Not content with saving lives on the front lines as a medic, Lifeline joined the Apex Games with hopes of securing more funding for the Corps.

Despite that sarcastic, nonchalant persona, Lifeline is a deeply caring person whose every act is selfless and fueled by kindness. Lifeline knows her actions in the Games cost lives, but to her the ends justify the means: her winnings will save more people than she eliminates.

PASSIVE — COMBAT MEDIC

Revive knocked-down teammates faster while protected by a shield wall. Also, all healing items are used 25% faster, meaning you will heal sooner than enemies.

TACTICAL — D.O.C. HEAL DRONE

Call your Drone of Compassion to automatically heal nearby teammates over time. Though it has small range, it helps conserve healing items.

ULTIMATE — CARE POD

Calls in a drop pod full of high-quality defensive gear. Upside: potential for very good armor. Downside: calls attention to your location.

Stick with your team:
Lifeline is best used in
group situations and
most of her abilities
are useless if you're
out on your own.

Care Packages are
loud. You can use one
as bait to disguise
your movements when
you know enemies
are approaching
your location.

Be attentive: The
boosted revives you
get mean you can
ourun enemy teams
in dogfights—and this
can be vital.

CLASS BREAKDOWN

MIRAGE

COCKY, TRICKY, AND ALWAYS WITH SOMETHING TO SAY, MIRAGE IS KNOWN FOR HIS CONFIDENCE SCAMS AND HOLOGRAPHIC DECEPTION.

Anyone who knows Mirage has probably heard him say something like, "I don't take myself too seriously. I don't take myself anywhere. I need to get out more," and that, really, is everything you need to know about him.

Mirage is the kind of person that likes attention—for all eyes to be on him. After his brothers went missing during the Frontier War, Mirage put his lifetime of training to use. He developed the tech his mother created for Holo-Pilots and made it better.

After spending a few years working in bars, listening to the locals talk up how good the Apex Games are, Mirage decided to enter (with his mother's blessing!). She even gave him the Holo-tech she'd been working on her whole career. Aw, bless.

Mirage now lives his best life, charming audiences and cheating opponents in the Apex Games.

PASSIVE — ENCORE!

Automatically drop a decoy and cloak for five seconds when knocked down. Not the best passive, but allows for quick pick-ups if the enemy isn't paying attention.

TACTICAL — PSYCH-OUT

Send out a holographic decoy to confuse the enemy. This is best used to distract and disorient enemies—fake out a push, then flank them.

ULTIMATE — VANISHING ACT

Deploy a team of Decoys to distract enemies while you cloak. A really good late-game ultimate, since it crowds the smaller rings and gives you a heads-up.

Mirage belongs on the front line. Get into the middle of the action, set up attacks and draw out foes with the hologram.

The ultimate is versatile and can be used to either escape unwinnable fights or put pressure on weakened teams.

Enemies reveal their location when they shoot Mirage's holograms. Poke fights to draw enemies out, then orchestrate team kills to finish them off.

OCTANE

A THRILL-SEEKING ADRENALINE JUNKIE WITH A TASTE FOR EXPLOSIVES, OCTANE BRINGS A WARPED SENSE OF FUN TO THE APEX GAMES.

Octavio Silva is the son of the preoccupied CEOs of Silva Pharmaceuticals—and he gets bored. He gets so bored, so often. Thanks to his privileged background, Silva often found himself wanting for nothing in life. To help address his chronic boredom, he would make daredevil videos and upload them for his myriad fans to enjoy across the planets.

One day, he had the bright idea of launching himself across the finish line with a grenade. It...didn't go as planned. The doctors amputated his legs and told him his days of being a stuntman were over. Instead, Silva enlisted the help of an old friend—Ajay Che, better known as Lifeline—and pressured her into replacing his broken legs with shiny new bionic ones.

Now able to repair his legs on the fly, Silva could chase bigger rushes than just silly stunts: he could enter the Apex Games and kill his boredom for good.

PASSIVE — SWIFT MEND

Automatically restores health over time. You regain one health every two seconds when not taking damage. It has great synergy with Stim, so don't be stingy with it.

TACTICAL — STIM

Move 30% faster for six seconds, but costs health to use. This is a great game-starting utility: Stimming after the jump gets you a head start on looting.

ULTIMATE — LAUNCH PAD

Deploy a jump pad that catapults teammates through the air. Really handy when trying to disengage from persistent foes or reach higher ground.

Launch Pads are best used before engaging with enemies, rather than in mid-battle. Make sure your team knows where the escape route is!

Playing Octane properly means you'll often get pinned by multiple enemies. Use Stim to speed up and get out. Then come back for more.

Octane is quick and can be hard to hit—use that risk/reward to your advantage and distract enemies as your allies set up kills.

PATHFINDER

PLAYFUL, UPBEAT, AND ALWAYS HAPPY TO HELP, PATHFINDER IS THE MOST WHOLESOME PRESENCE IN THE APEX GAMES.

Pathfinder is a MRVN (Mobile Robotic Versatile eNtity) who has been modified to specialize in surveying the environment and scouting the often uncharted lands ahead of missions in the Outlands. Rumors have it that the friendly robot booted up decades ago in an abandoned laboratory. He had no idea who created him, or indeed why he was created.

With only his MRVN designation to hint at his identity, Pathfinder set off to do what he is so good at doing: scouting for his creator. Since he began his journey, Pathfinder has learned a lot. He's learned a lot about food (his favorite dish to make is the Eastern Leviathan Stew), but he's still at a loss as to who made him.

Pathfinder is canny. He knows that if he can gain enough notoriety in the Apex Games, he can perhaps get famous enough to draw the attention of his creator.

PASSIVE — INSIDER KNOWLEDGE

Scan a survey beacon to reveal the ring's next location—a very useful ability if you want to get ahead of the game and start laying traps for incoming players.

TACTICAL — GRAPPLING HOOK

Grapple to get to out-of-reach places quickly. Used to flee enemies and navigate around the map, and useful for staying out of sight until you're ready to engage.

ULTIMATE — ZIP LINE GUN

Keep an eye out for players that stray from their teams. Pathfinder can use this ultimate to flank them and pick off loners.

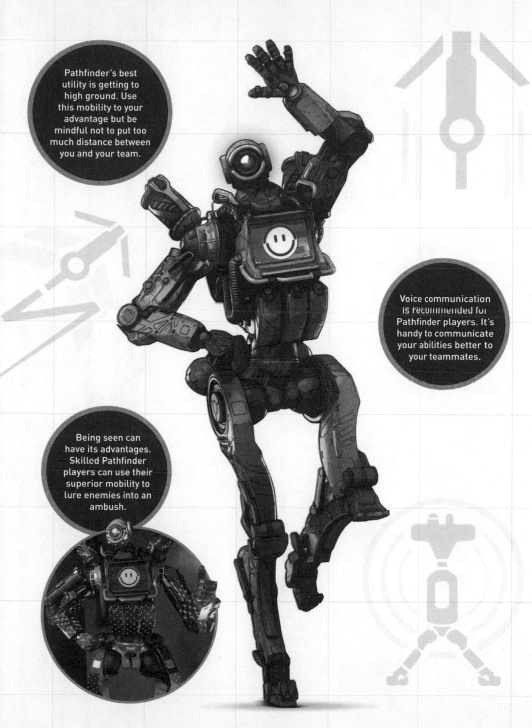

Pathfinder's best utility is getting to high ground. Use this mobility to your advantage but be mindful not to put too much distance between you and your team.

Voice communication is recommended for Pathfinder players. It's handy to communicate your abilities better to your teammates.

Being seen can have its advantages. Skilled Pathfinder players can use their superior mobility to lure enemies into an ambush.

WRAITH

INTERDIMENSIONAL SKIRMISHER WRAITH IS A TROUBLED BUT EXCELLENT WARRIOR, PLAGUED BY HER PAST BUT SET ON HER FUTURE.

Wraith has a command of the battlefield that other combatants can only dream of: the terrifying ability to rend space and time and open rifts in reality. This makes her a whirlwind fighter, a rapid, unpredictable enemy…but she has no idea how she gained these powers.

Wraith woke up in an IMC Detention Facility for the mentally ill years ago, and she remembered nothing. She had no clue how she got to where she was, or what her life had been before. The only thing she knew was the distant voice whispering in her mind, the voice that would starve her of sleep and challenge her sanity.

Determined to uncover her true identity, Wraith learned to listen to the voice, and it started to tell her how to use her powers. The facilities that were used to experiment on her are buried under the Apex Games arenas, so Wraith is here with a score to settle.

PASSIVE — VOICES FROM THE VOID

A voice warns you when danger approaches. As far as you can tell, it's on your side. Effective in solo play and groups—as long as you communicate!

TACTICAL — INTO THE VOID

Reposition quickly through the safety of void space, avoiding all damage. This is a handy ability to use to sneak up and assassinate enemies.

ULTIMATE — DIMENSIONAL RIFT

Link two locations with portals for 60 seconds, allowing your entire team to use them. You're left vulnerable, but it can help teammates get out of bad situations.

Lots of clutch plays come down to Wraith's ability to teleport and escape: she's a late-game hero. Watch out for enemy Wraiths when it gets down to the final few squads.

Wraith is best put to use for situational awareness. Sneaking around and highlighting enemies for your team should be a priority.

When attacking enemies at long to medium range, set up a portal for your team to escape through. This aids regrouping, and draws out attackers, too.

BUILDING THE PERFECT SQUAD

THE GAME'S HEROES MAKE IT UNIQUE, AND MASTERING HOW THEY ALL WORK TOGETHER IS VITAL TO YOUR VICTORY.

SNEAKY SMOKE AND SIGHT

BLOODHOUND, BANGALORE, WRAITH

By leveraging one of the most powerful tactical abilities in the game (Bangalore's smoke grenade) with a player that can see through smoke (Bloodhound), you can theoretically wipe out entire teams without even being detected. Use Wraith to portal up and send in Bloodhound, and you're onto a winner.

THE BAIT & SWITCH

GIBRALTAR, MIRAGE, WRAITH

By utilizing Gibraltar's Tactical dome-shield and Wraith's ultimate dimensional rift, you can lead enemy teams into a dangerous situation. They'll come to the dome, expecting to pressure you, and find it empty. Then you can come around on them, pop Mirage's ultimate to disorient them more, and punish.

PURE AGGRESSION

BLOODHOUND, PATHFINDER, BANGALORE

If you want to be in the thick of the action, this is the team for you. Smart players can use Bloodhound to track enemies and intercept them, Pathfinder can create quick routes to where they're headed, and Bangalore can smoke them before they know what's happening. Play it smart, and play two steps ahead.

TROJAN HORSE

GIBRALTAR, LIFELINE, CAUSTIC

A team for more passive players. If you consistently get to the end game and fall down there, this may be for you. Use Lifeline to heal allies in Gibraltar's shield, and use Caustic's gas to keep enemies at bay. The shield can also be useful when Lifeline calls in packages to make sure you don't get rushed.

THE SPEEDRUNNERS

OCTANE, WRAITH, MIRAGE

This is a team that causes headaches for enemies: Wraith, Octane, and Mirage are all tricky to pin down and fire on. Keep escaping and breaking the enemy's line of sight. Consider baiting enemy teams into each other and picking off the survivors, coaxing them out with Mirage's holograms.

THE SURVIVALISTS

PATHFINDER, BLOODHOUND, MIRAGE

This build focuses on outliving other teams by avoiding the front lines. Pathfinder's passive tells you where the next ring will be, so you can head in and use Bloodhound's tracker to avoid other teams. Mirage's ultimate should buy you time if you get spotted. Pilfer, loot, and get the best items until you're forced to fight.

RING CLOSING ///

YOU ARE THE

CHAMPION

◀))ItsKorvyy

PINGS

THE PING SYSTEM HELPS SET APEX LEGENDS APART FROM ITS PEERS. IT'S A UNIQUE MECHANIC, AND ONE THAT TAKES TIME TO MASTER.

Apex Legends immediately stood out from the battle royale crowd by introducing the "Ping" system to the game. Mapped to the right bumper on consoles and to the mouse wheel on PC, the Ping system is an ingenious way for players to call attention to items in-game, even without using voice chat. By including a system like this in a battle royale game, Respawn has effectively lowered the barrier of entry for the title, revolutionizing the whole genre.

Pings cover many actions, from marking enemies to announcing the location of loot bins, from calling "dibs" on distant booty to telling teammates where you want the team to travel.

Pinging not only calls attention to something in-game via a dedicated voice line from your character, it'll also pop up as a text message in the chat and mark a location on your teammates' HUD—both super-simple features that are incredibly valuable in practice. Never forget to ping: it can be the difference between life and death.

ATTACKING HERE

DEFENDING THIS AREA

ENEMY

GO / GOING HERE

LOOTING HERE

SOMEONE'S BEEN HERE

WATCHING HERE

DO

Respond to other players' pings. How will your allies know you've acknowledged their location suggestion if you don't respond? Be polite.

DO

Ping from your inventory. If you need more of any specific ammo, you can hover over it in your screen and hit the ping button. Don't be afraid to ask.

DO

Ping enemy locations. All the time. Even if they're as far away as can be. Having that blip on the map could save your life one day.

DO

Ping loot caches, even late in the game. You never know who's less decked-out than you and may need that Blue Helmet, even in round four!

DON'T

Spam pings. It's all well and good repeatedly pinging "Mozambique here," but doing it while an ally is listening for enemy steps could cost you the game.

DON'T

Hoard items. If your teammate is requesting shields or health, you can drop them from your inventory. Three players are always better than two.

DON'T

Forget to ping when you're knocked down. A downed player has good eyes on the action and you pinging an enemy's location could save a life.

DON'T

Forget to cancel. Pings can interfere with a player's HUD, and a forgotten location ping on-screen could be a crucial distraction that proves fatal.

REVIVING & RESPAWNING

LEARN HOW TO BRING YOUR TEAM BACK FROM THE JAWS OF DEFEAT AND YOU'LL BE THE BEST APEX LEGENDS COMEBACK KID THERE EVER WAS.

KNOW HOW TO REVIVE

Apex Legends is unique among battle royale games thanks to its respawn mechanic. To bring allies back, you'll need to recover their banner from the loot box they drop when they die, then head to a Respawn Beacon. A drop ship will soon come and deliver your ally back into the game.

BE A GOOD DOWNED ALLY

If you die, you'll be able to watch the camera of one of your teammates, or hang around your dropped banner for a while. Here, you can act as a lookout, speaking to your teammates and letting them know the locations of incoming threats.

GET YOURSELF UP!

If you're lucky enough to find a Gold tier (level 4) backpack out in the wild, you'll gain the ability to self-revive. This takes a little while to charge but can be a very handy form of deceit when you get knocked; scramble to safety and ambush an unsuspecting enemy.

KNOW YOUR TIMES

The first time you get knocked down in a game, it will take you 90 seconds to bleed out. The second time you get knocked down, it will take you 60 seconds. Respawning at a Beacon will reset these times—always remember that!

FIDDLE WITH THE HUD

When a teammate is knocked down or killed, an icon will appear on your HUD: red for knocked, green for eliminated. These big icons can be a pain—you can head to Settings, then Gameplay tab, and then set Ping Opacity to Faded to make this a bit less intrusive when you're playing.

DON'T FORGET TO SHARE

Respawned teammates come back with no gear at all. If it's late in the game, try and locate nearby death boxes brimming with loot. Alternatively, don't be afraid to drop your own guns: two players with a weapon each are better than a fully naked, vulnerable player.

BE QUICK OR BE DEAD

Once killed, a downed ally's banner hangs around for only about 90 seconds, so make a dash to get the banner or that ally will be out of the game entirely. Sometimes risking it to grab the banner and revive an ally is worth it!

LOOTING

AS WITH ANY BATTLE ROYALE, SUCCESS IN APEX LEGENDS CAN HINGE ON WHAT—AND HOW—YOU LOOT.

LOOT TIERS

To understand the best items to loot and pick up, you need to know what you're looking for. First of all, here are the different tiers of loot in *Apex Legends*.

 COMMON   EPIC

 RARE   LEGENDARY

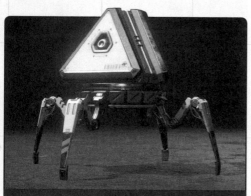

LOOT TICKS

Hidden across the maps, spawning in different places in different matches, you'll find Loot Ticks. These are identical to the Apex Crates you'll open from the main menu, and are often found in built-up locations.

Listen up when you're looting areas with buildings. You can hear them bleeping and blooping, so make sure to sniff around corners and on top of platforms if you hear some strange robotic noises.

WHAT TO LOOK FOR

With any loot, you're going to want to look for the best colors. Gold Legendary items give you top-tier stats, as well as bonus benefits. The earlier you get these items, the better your chance of survival.

HIGH PRIORITY!

Occasionally, you'll find "gold" versions of weapons that come fully equipped with best-in-class attachments. Usually found in Hot Zones, these weapons will massively improve your chances in the early- to mid-game.

DON'T BE SELFISH

Apex Legends is a team game, so you don't need to take everything yourself. Remember to ping your teammates with loot locations—you never know who's going to be more effective with any given loot item than you are.

LOOT TYPES

There are a lot of different types of loot to find in the game. Breaking them down into different categories is vital if you want to best understand how to take advantage of them.

WEAPON ATTACHMENTS

SNIPER STOCK
Improves the handling speed and idle sway

STANDARD STOCK
Improves rifle or SMG handling speed and idle sway

EXTENDED LIGHT MAG
Increases ammo size for light guns

EXTENDED HEAVY MAG
Increases ammo size for heavy guns

HOP-UPS
Changes how a weapon operates and works

BARREL STABILIZERS
Decreases recoil for many different weapons

SHOTGUN BOLT
Increases shotgun fire rate

OPTICS

Digital Threat: Highlights enemies

Digital Sniper Threat: Highlights enemies, variable zoom

3x HCOG "Ranger": Variable zoom. For Sniper Rifles, LMGs, ARs, SMGs

2x-4x Variable AOG: Variable zoom. For Sniper Rifles, LMGs, ARs, SMGs

4x-8x Variable Sniper: Variable zoom. For Sniper Rifles

2x HCOG 'Bruiser': For all guns

6x Sniper: For Snipers

1x-2x Variable Holo: Variable zoom. All guns

1x Holo: All guns

1x HCOG "Classic": All guns

ARMOR

Body Shield (Level 4)
+100 Shield Capacity. Full shield recharge when you execute knocked enemies

Helmet (Level 4)
25% damage reduction. Increases Tactical, ultimate recharge speed

Knockdown Shield (Level 4)
750 Health Knockdown Shield. Allows self-revive on knockdown

Backpack (Level 4)
Adds 6 inventory slots. Doubles speed of healing items

Body Shield (Level 3)
+100 Shield Capacity

Helmet (Level 3)
25% damage reduction

Knockdown Shield (Level 3)
750 Health Knockdown Shield

Backpack (Level 3)
Adds 6 inventory slots

Body Shield (Level 2)
+75 Shield Capacity

Helmet (Level 2)
20% damage reduction

Knockdown Shield (Level 2)
250 Health Knockdown Shield

Backpack (Level 2)
Adds 4 inventory slots

Body Shield (Level 1)
+50 Shield Capacity

Helmet (Level 1)
10% damage reduction

Knockdown Shield (Level 1)
100 Health Knockdown Shield

Backpack (Level 1)
Adds 2 inventory slots

PISTOLS

THE MOST VERSATILE GUNS IN THE GAME ARE ALSO THE EASIEST TO FIND.

Pistols are notable for their handling: if you're a mobile, quick player, try and master the Wingman. It goes well with good Octane, Mirage, and Pathfinder players.

WINGMAN

The most powerful and popular gun in the early days of *Apex Legends*, the Wingman is every run-and-gunner's best friend. Modeled on a classic revolver, the handgun can take down opponents in three shots (if you've got good aim), and if you can handle the weighty kick, it can carry you to victory every time.

AMMO TYPE	MAG SIZE	DPS
HEAVY	DEFAULT: 6 / LEVEL 3: 12	[BODY] 45 / [HEAD] 90
PROS		CONS
CAN QUICKLY TAKE OUT ENEMIES IN THE EARLY GAME		KICKS LIKE A MULE
HEADSHOTS PACK A LETHAL PUNCH		APPALLING ACCURACY FROM THE HIP

TOP ATTACHMENT
SKULLPIERCER RIFLING
INCREASES HEADSHOT DAMAGE BY OVER 2X

TOP ATTACHMENT
DIGITAL THREAT

RE-45

AMMO TYPE	MAG SIZE	DPS
LIGHT	DEFAULT 15 / LEVEL 3: 24	[BODY] 11 / [HEAD] 16
PROS		CONS
TIGHT BULLET SPREAD, EASY TO FOCUS FIRE		SMALL MAGAZINE, QUICHLY NEED TO RELOAD
QUICK AND MOBILE HANDLING		QUICHLY OUTCLASSED BY HIGHER-TIER GUNS

P2020

AMMO TYPE	MAG SIZE	DPS
LIGHT	DEFAULT: 10 / LEVEL 3: 18	[BODY] 12 / [HEAD] 18
PROS		CONS
TIGHT, PREDICTABLE BULLET SPREAD		LOW OVERALL DAMAGE OUTPUT
GOOD FOR HOLDING WEAPON ATTACHMENTS		SEMI-AUTOMATIC IS OUTCLASSED BY FULLY AUTOMATIC WEAPONS

SHOTGUNS

CLOSE-RANGE EXPERTS AND TRAP LAYERS: SHOTGUNS ARE YOUR BEST ALLIES.

MASTIFF

A legendary shotgun found only in airdrops, there's a reason this weapon only comes with 20 ammo pre-loaded. The semi-automatic monster can chew through even Legendary-tier body armor with ease. If you see an enemy with this, engage from afar.

AMMO TYPE	MAG SIZE	DPS
UNIQUE	DEFAULT: 4	[BODY] UP TO 188 / [HEAD] UP TO 288
PROS		CONS
CAN PRETTY MUCH ONE-SHOT FOES, EARLY- TO MID-GAME		VERY SMALL AMMO CLIP
NEGLIGIBLE RECOIL MAKES IT EASY TO USE		ONE OF THE RAREST GUNS IN THE GAME

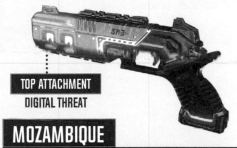

TOP ATTACHMENT
DIGITAL THREAT

MOZAMBIQUE

AMMO TYPE	MAG SIZE	DPS
SHOTGUN	DEFAULT 3	[BODY] UP TO 45 / [HEAD] UP TO 66
PROS		CONS
RELATIVELY FAST RATE OF FIRE		APPALLING DAMAGE OUTPUT FOR SHOTGUN CLASS
QUICK, RESPONSIVE HANDLING		TERRIBLE MAGAZINE SIZE

TOP ATTACHMENT
PRECISION CHOKE

PEACEKEEPER

AMMO TYPE	MAG SIZE	DPS
SHOTGUN	DEFAULT: 6	[BODY] UP TO 110 / [HEAD] UP TO 165
PROS		CONS
VERY HIGH DAMAGE OUTPUT IF ALL BULLETS HIT		BASE WEAPON HAS LOW RATE OF FIRE
EVEN DEADLIER WITH PRECISION CHOKE		LIMITED MAGAZINE SIZE

EVA-8 AUTO

TOP ATTACHMENT
LEGENDARY SHOTGUN BOLT

AMMO TYPE	MAG SIZE	DPS
SHOTGUN	DEFAULT 8	[BODY] UP TO 63 / [HEAD] UP TO 90
PROS		CONS
HIGH DAMAGE POTENTIAL		UNPREDICTABLE BULLET SPREAD
DEADLY IN PRACTICED HANDS		NOT VERY CUSTOMIZABLE

SMGs

IF YOU WANT TO SUPPRESS CLOSE-RANGE ENEMIES, SMGs ARE FOR YOU.

R-99

The R-99 will most likely be one of the first weapons you pick up after you drop, and something you'll take at least until mid-game. It's reliable and customizable, and it provides decent damage output from close- to mid-range. Learn to use this weapon, and you'll be able to survive the early-game feeding frenzy with ease.

TOP ATTACHMENT
LEGENDARY BARREL STABILIZER

A good SMG player will prioritize upgrading the magazine: you can dish out pretty good damage per second with SMGs, but only if you have enough bullets!

AMMO TYPE	MAG SIZE		DPS
LIGHT	DEFAULT: 18 / LEVEL 3: 30		[BODY] 12 / [HEAD] 18
PROS		CONS	
RAPID RATE OF FIRE		LOWEST DAMAGE OF ALL SMGs	
HIGH MAGAZINE CAPACITY		NEEDS ATTACHMENTS TO BE *REALLY* GOOD	

TOP ATTACHMENT
SELECTFIRE RECEIVER

PROWLER BURST PDW

AMMO TYPE	MAG SIZE	DPS
HEAVY	DEFAULT: 20 / LEVEL 3: 35	[BODY] UP TO 70 PER BURST / [HEAD] UP TO 105 PER BURST
PROS		CONS
WITH FULLY AUTOMATIC FIRE, CAN DEAL GREAT DAMAGE		BURST FIRE ISN'T AMAZING, NEEDS HOP-UP TO BE VALID
SUITS A VARIETY OF PLAYSTYLES		RECOIL IS VERY HARD TO MASTER

TOP ATTACHMENT
DIGITAL THREAT

ALTERNATOR SMG

AMMO TYPE	MAG SIZE	DPS
LIGHT	DEFAULT: 16 / LEVEL 3: 26	[BODY] 13 / [HEAD] 19
PROS		CONS
SMALL, LIGHT, EASY TO USE		LOW DAMAGE OUTPUT
PREDICTABLE VERTICAL RECOIL PATTERN		USELESS WITHOUT MULTIPLE ATTACHMENTS

FIRING RANGE

LMGs

IN THE RIGHT HANDS, LMGs CAN TAKE DOWN AN ENTIRE TEAM.

M600 SPITFIRE

TOP ATTACHMENT
LEGENDARY BARREL STABILIZER

The whole LMG class can lay down big damage—but at the cost of mobility. Though both LMGs are particularly dangerous, the Spitfire comes out on top of the Devotion because of its massive damage per shot, huge Level 3 magazine size, and ferocity at more or less every range.

AMMO TYPE	MAG SIZE	DPS	
LIGHT	DEFAULT: 35 / LEVEL 3: 60	[BODY] 20 / [HEAD] 40	
PROS		CONS	
VERY HIGH DAMAGE PER SHOT		SLOW TO RELOAD AND READY UP	
VERY HIGH MAGAZINE CAPACITY		FIRE RATE CHUGS—NOT IDEAL WITH ZIGZAG RECOIL	

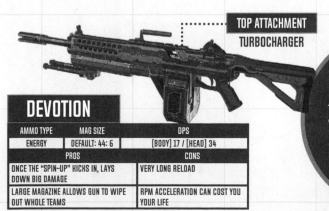

TOP ATTACHMENT
TURBOCHARGER

DEVOTION

AMMO TYPE	MAG SIZE	DPS	
ENERGY	DEFAULT: 44: 6	[BODY] 17 / [HEAD] 34	
PROS		CONS	
ONCE THE "SPIN-UP" KICKS IN, LAYS DOWN BIG DAMAGE		VERY LONG RELOAD	
LARGE MAGAZINE ALLOWS GUN TO WIPE OUT WHOLE TEAMS		RPM ACCELERATION CAN COST YOU YOUR LIFE	

If you want to master LMGs, be sure to always keep context in mind. A Devotion dressed up with a Turbocharger can quickly put entire enemy teams to bed in the smaller rings, whereas a Spitfire with a big magazine can be a very handy gun to keep enemies at bay as you beat a tactical retreat.

FIRING RANGE

ARs

EASY TO USE, EASY TO FIND, AND EASY TO MASTER— AN IDEAL WEAPON CLASS FOR BEGINNERS.

R-301

TOP ATTACHMENT
EPIC EXTENDED LIGHT MAG

This weapon, which can be found everywhere in the game, is a good all-purpose option in *Apex Legends*. Using the most common ammo in the game, and laying down double the damage with a headshot, this weapon is a perfect all-rounder and will be useful even when you're down to the final few teams.

AMMO TYPE	MAG SIZE		DPS
LIGHT	DEFAULT: 18 / LEVEL 3: 28		[BODY] 14 / [HEAD] 28
	PROS	CONS	
HIGH ACCURACY AND HIGH RATE OF FIRE		LOW BASE DAMAGE	
ONE OF THE BEST LONG-RANGE RIFLES		LOW BASE MAGAZINE SIZE	

TOP ATTACHMENT
EPIC EXTENDED HEAVY MAG

VK-47 FLATLINE

AMMO TYPE	MAG SIZE	DPS
HEAVY	DEFAULT: 20 / LEVEL 3: 30	[BODY] 16 / [HEAD] 32
PROS		CONS
HIGH BASE DAMAGE, DOUBLED ON HEADSHOT		POOR ACCURACY AND HIGH, UNPREDICTABLE RECOIL
GREAT AT CLOSE AND MEDIUM RANGE		USELESS AT LONG RANGE

TOP ATTACHMENT
EPIC EXTENDED HEAVY MAG

HEMLOCK BURST AR

AMMO TYPE	MAG SIZE	DPS
HEAVY	DEFAULT: 18 / LEVEL	[BODY] 18 / [HEAD] 36
PROS		CONS
HIGH ACCURACY, AND GREAT DAMAGE IF ALL THREE BULLETS HIT		LOW BASE RATE OF FIRE AND MAGAZINE CAPACITY
SATISFYING RATE OF FIRE AT MEDIUM TO LONG RANGE		POOR CHOICE FOR CLOSE-RANGE ENCOUNTERS

TOP ATTACHMENT
TURBOCHARGER

HAVOC RIFLE

AMMO TYPE	MAG SIZE	DPS
ENERGY	DEFAULT: 25	[BODY] 18 / [HEAD] 36
PROS		CONS
HIGH DAMAGE PER SECOND FOR AR CLASS		PRETTY HARD TO USE AND MASTER WITHOUT TURBOCHARGER
VERSATILE, GOOD FOR DIFFERENT CONTEXTS		RARE AMMO TYPE

SNIPER RIFLES

THERE'S NOTHING MORE SATISFYING THAN TAKING SOMEONE OUT FROM HALF A MAP AWAY.

KЯABER

Though it can deliver a massive 250 headshot damage—capable of wiping out an opponent in one shot—this weapon requires an expert to use it properly. Landing in the game with only eight ammo, a masterful sniper can pick off whole enemy teams before they even know where you are. Just make sure you're quick—and accurate.

AMMO TYPE	MAG SIZE	DPS	
UNIQUE	DEFAULT: 4	[BODY] 125 / [HEAD] 250	
PROS		CONS	
TOP-IN-GAME DAMAGE ON HEADSHOTS		COMES WITH VERY LITTLE AMMO	
BODY SHOTS CAPABLE OF DOWNING UNDER-EQUIPPED ENEMIES		ONLY USEFUL FOR LONG-RANGE ENCOUNTERS	

TOP ATTACHMENT
DIGITAL SNIPER THREAT

G7 SCOUT

AMMO TYPE	MAG SIZE	DPS	
LIGHT	DEFAULT: 10 / LEVEL 3: 20	[BODY] 30 / [HEAD] 60	
PROS		CONS	
HIGHEST SNIPER RATE OF FIRE		WATCH OUT FOR THE GLOWING IRON SIGHT	
GREAT FOR HEADSHOTS AND POTSHOTS AT RANGE		LOTS OF HARD, VERTICAL RECOIL	

TOP ATTACHMENT
SKULLPIERCER RIFLING

LONGBOW DMR

AMMO TYPE	MAG SIZE	DPS	
HEAVY	DEFAULT: 5 / LEVEL 3: 10	[BODY] 55 / [HEAD] 110	
PROS		CONS	
MASSIVE DAMAGE PER SHOT		TERRIBLE HIP FIRE ACCURACY AND PREDICTABILITY	
CAN DOWN INJURED ENEMIES FROM AFAR		ATTACHMENTS DON'T CROP UP TOO OFTEN	

TOP ATTACHMENT
PRECISION CHOKE

TRIPLE TAKE

AMMO TYPE	MAG SIZE	DPS	
ENERGY	DEFAULT: 5	[BODY] 69 IF ALL HIT / [HEAD] 138 IF ALL HIT	
PROS		CONS	
THREE SHOTS WITH A TIGHT SPREAD MAKE IT HARD TO MISS		LOW MAGAZINE, CAN'T BE UPGRADED	
IF ALL THREE BULLETS HIT, THERE'S GREAT DAMAGE POTENTIAL		NEEDS SKULLPIERCER TO LAY DOWN DECENT CRITICAL DAMAGE	

TRAPS & STEALTH

SURVIVING AND OUTLASTING OTHER PLAYERS IN APEX LEGENDS IS KEY TO GETTING TO THE ENDGAME. AND WHEN YOU'RE THERE, YOU NEED TO PLAY DIRTY.

NOX NOX, WHO'S THERE?

PLAN

Caustic's Tactical Nox Grenades are solid items—they block doors. In places like Slums and Bunker, you can lock enemy teams in rooms and watch them suck up damage until they're doomed…a nasty play.

SET UP

Follow an enemy team into a tight area—this works anywhere with one or two doors sealing off a room. Keep your teammates on point to flank.

EXECUTE

If the whole team is in a room, pop your Tacticals down—two on each door. This will trap enemies in, and if they crack a door or try to shoot their way out, they'll trigger the canisters. Try throwing down a grenade for good measure, too.

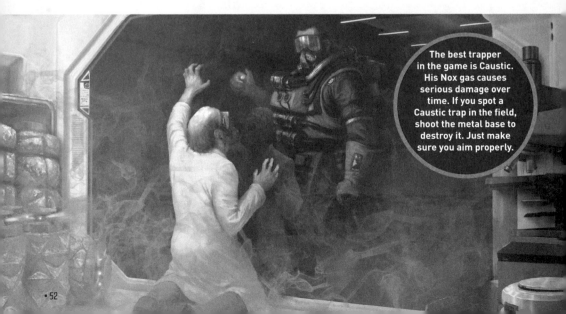

The best trapper in the game is Caustic. His Nox gas causes serious damage over time. If you spot a Caustic trap in the field, shoot the metal base to destroy it. Just make sure you aim properly.

GET OVER HERE!

PLAN

Pathfinder's tactical Grapple can pull enemies in. So lay good guns or purple loot down on bridges in areas like Swamps, where you can fall off the map. This is an unexpected play.

SET UP

Head to an area where enemies can fall off the map: Runway, Swamps, anywhere at the edge of the map.

EXECUTE

Bait other players with some enticing loot, then Grapple them from behind, sending them plummeting.

NOW YOU'RE THINKING WITH PORTALS

PLAN

Wraith's ultimate portal is one of the most useful defensive abilities in the game, but this trick is a more aggressive use of the power.

SET UP

Get your whole team hidden in a room or small, enclosed area. Keep an eye on your flanks and head somewhere open to trigger your ultimate.

EXECUTE

Run back to your team. If you know there's a target out there, wait behind the portal entrance. A disoriented enemy will emerge and get a back full of buckshot if all goes according to plan. Sometimes even works to wipeout entire teams.

Different areas have different properties when it comes to movement and sound. Walking through water under wooden buildings is noisier than walking through grass, for example. The quicker you move, the more noise you make. The best Legends are silent.

SURVIVING THE ENDGAME

THIS IS WHAT YOU'VE BEEN TRAINING FOR: THE ONE-ON-ONES, THE CLUTCH PLAYS, THE MOMENTS OF GLORY. YOU'VE GOT THIS.

The endgame is where *Apex Legends* really comes into its own. It's where all elements of speed, ferocity, judgement, and teamwork collide, leaving you in the smallest ring with nothing but one or two other teams keeping you from victory. It's tense, it's sweaty, and it's hard—and it's easy to lose your head.

There are two schools of thought on the endgame: rushing and camping. Do you prefer to wait out the attacks of an oncoming team, or try and get the drop on them? All the heroes' abilities come into focus in these last few seconds, with some (Lifeline's, Pathfinder's) becoming less while others (Mirage's, Bangalore's) become game-changing.

Examine your surroundings, know what healing items and projectiles you have on hand, and remember the strengths and weaknesses of the guns you're carrying. That should stand you in good enough stead to enter the fight and come out victorious.

DO

Flank. Outmaneuvering enemies at this stage is vital. Use two players to draw out enemies, and the third can diverge and flank their position, often to devastating effect.

DO

Use your abilities. The action gets quicker when the ring is bearing down on you, but your abilities will still recharge. Late-game success requires risk to get reward, so pull out all the stops.

DO

Remember to loot death boxes. By the late game, recently downed players will have top-tier loot: make sure to capitalize on this. Take Phoenix Kits and recharge shields when possible.

DO

Use your throwables. Arc Stars, Thermite Grenades, and Frags can be really good for cornering and weakening enemies. Block escape routes with Arcs and Thermite, and take some potshots.

DON'T

Let the ring hem you in. Yes, in the later rounds it does do a lot of damage, but you can rush opponents from an angle they aren't expecting if you play smart and fast outside of the ring.

DON'T

Camp in buildings. *Apex* is a game that favors movement and speed—make sure you put pressure on the enemy, know where your next piece of cover is, and push for it when you can.

DON'T

Get pinned in low ground. If you are going to camp, then camp high and be vigilant. Don't let the appeal of gaining speed by sliding downhill get you cornered and trapped.

DON'T

Just rush in. It can be tempting to try and "Leeroy Jenkins" the final seconds of a match, but that will only leave you and your team out of sync, out of cover, and out of luck. Play it cool, until the end.

ADVANCED TIPS

THERE ARE A LOT OF LITTLE TRICKS IN APEX LEGENDS THAT WON'T BE IMMEDIATELY OBVIOUS. LET US FIX THAT FOR YOU.

Apex Legends **is absolutely riddled with little character tips and quirks that you only really get to know about by playing a lot.** We've been experimenting with this game more or less since it launched in order to sniff out some of the sneakiest, most vital pieces of information you wouldn't otherwise get to know.

Listed below is a rapid-fire list of some of the best bits of knowledge we've picked up over hundreds of hours of play. We hope it helps.

Octane's Tactical—Stim—will never take you below 1 health. If you're near death, you may as well be quick!

Doors take two kicks to break down, but if you time it with a teammate, you can knock them in one. Good for ambushes.

Bloodhound can transform into his ultimate immediately when on a zip line, meaning you can be combat ready if coming in hot.

You can slide backward as quickly as you can slide forward. Worth bearing in mind when you're retreating from incoming enemies.

Jump Kicking (jump then melee) has a quicker cooldown than regular melee, meaning you can chain more and do more damage by using this technique.

Caustic players should prioritize Thermite Grenades: the damage they do combines with his Nox clouds to rapidly drain the health of anyone caught in both.

Wraith's portals block doors. Want to hide some time to heal, or create a diversion away from your allies? Wraith can surprise you.

Want a mobile bulletproof base? Deploy Lifeline's D.O.C., then pop Gibraltar's dome-shield on top and voila! You can move it as you push forward.

Never aim down sights with shotguns: it takes time and they're cumbersome. Hip fire will usually have the same effect in less time.

Peacekeeper shotguns can be fired "twice." Fire, reload, switch weapon, then switch back. This whole cycle is quicker than reloading, and can devastate close-range enemies.

Wraith's portals last 60 seconds, but Respawn didn't include a timer... or did they? If you see 39% on your ultimate charge, your portal is about to disappear.

Don't accidentally die by standing on confined supply bins as they open, or by standing under Supply Drops: both can squish you, bringing instant death.

Reloading while there is still ammo in your clip is faster than a full reload on 90% of weapons in the game.

Generally speaking, it's better to swap out your Body Shield than heal up your current one. It saves time and keeps healing items in your inventory for when you might really need them.

If you have a Lifeline on your team, always give them the ultimate accelerant—it's the slowest charging ultimate in the game and provides the best rewards.

Finishers look good, but they're not practical. They don't all take the same amount of time, either: the shortest is four seconds and the longest is just over six.

BATTLE PASS

THE INAUGURAL SEASON OF APEX LEGENDS FEATURED A TON OF UPGRADES AND ITEMS TO COLLECT. CHECK OFF YOUR BATTLE PASS REWARDS HERE.

***Apex Legends* allows players to buy a Battle Pass every season, which grants access to 100 bonus rewards (on top of whatever you get out of Apex Packs).**

As well as the 100 paid rewards, there are also 24 free rewards players can earn per season without paying for the Battle Pass. The rewards

earned from the Battle Pass each season are exclusive, and won't be made available again after the season has ended, so if you want everything, you have to play a lot!

Each Battle Pass lasts about three months, but be aware that Respawn could change timescales and pricing at any time in the future.

LEVEL	REWARD	FREE REWARD
1	Revolutionary Lifeline Skin, Outlaw Mirage Skin, Survivor Wraith Skin	–
2	Harvest Triple Take Skin	Apex Pack
3	Wraith Tracker—Season 1 Kills	–
4	Patchwork Hemlock Skin	Gibraltar Tracker—Season 1 Wins
5	Wild Frontier Level Badge	–
6	Opening Season Bangalore Quip	Pathfinder Tracker—Season 1 Wins
7	50 Apex Coins	–
8	Bloodhound Tracker—Season 1 Kills	Wraith Tracker—Season 1 Wins
9	Navigator Prowler Skin	–
10	Wild Frontier Level Badge	Bangalore Tracker—Season 1 Wins
11	50 Apex Coins	–
12	BP Point Boost: +5% survival time as BP per squad member	Apex Pack
13	Funny Bones Mirage Frame	–
14	Navigator Longbow Skin	Bloodhound Tracker—Season 1 Wins
15	Wild Frontier Level Badge	–

LEVEL	REWARD	FREE REWARD
16	Opening Season Mirage Quip	Caustic Tracker—Season 1 Wins
17	50 Apex Coins	–
18	Flight Risk Octane Frame	Mirage Tracker—Season 1 Wins
19	Patchwork Spitfire Skin	–
20	Wild Frontier Level Badge	Lifeline Tracker—Season 1 Wins
21	50 Apex Coins	–
22	BP Point Boost: +2.5% survival time as BP per squad member	Octane Tracker—Season 1 Wins
23	Silk Road Wraith Frame	–
24	Navigator Mozambique Skin	Apex Pack

LEVEL	REWARD	FREE REWARD	LEVEL	REWARD	FREE REWARD
25	Wild Frontier Level Badge	–	60	Wild Frontier Level Badge	–
26	Epic Apex Pack	Caustic Tracker—Season 1 Damage	61	Pick Me Up Lifeline Frame	–
27	Season Opening Pathfinder Quip	–	62	BP Point Boost: +2.5% survival time as BP per squad member	–
28	Mirage Tracker—Season 1 Kills	Bangalore Tracker—Season 1 Damage	63	100 Apex Coins	–
29	Harvest Kraber Skin	–	64	Harvest P2020 Skin	–
30	Wild Frontier Level Badge	Gibraltar Tracker—Season 1 Damage	65	Wild Frontier Level Badge	–
31	50 Apex Coins	–	66	Opening Season Bloodhound Quip	–
32	BP Point Boost: +2.5% survival time as BP per squad member	Bloodhound Tracker—Season 1 Damage	67	100 Apex Coins	–
33	Pathfinder Tracker—Season 1 Kills	–	68	Lifeline Tracker—Season 1 Kills	–
34	Patchwork EVA Skin	Apex Pack	69	Patchwork Havoc Skin	–
35	Wild Frontier Level Badge	–	70	Wild Frontier Level Badge	–
36	Opening Season Caustic Quip	Lifeline Tracker – Season 1 Damage	71	Knock Down Bloodhound Frame	–
37	50 Apex Coins	–	72	BP Point Boost: +2.5% survival time as BP per squad member	–
38	Caustic Tracker—Season 1 Kills	Octane Tracker—Season 1 Damage	73	Apex Pack	–
39	Navigator Flatline Skin	–	74	Harvest R-99 Skin	–
40	Wild Frontier Level Badge	Wraith Tracker—Season 1 Damage	75	Wild Frontier Level Badge	–
41	50 Apex Coins	–	76	Open Season Octane Quip	–
42	BP Point Boost: +2.5% survival time as BP per squad member	Mirage Tracker—Season 1 Damage	77	100 Apex Coins	–
43	Apex Pack	–	78	Bangalore Tracker—Season 1 Kills	–
44	Patchwork Alternator Skin	Pathfinder Tracker—Season 1 Damage	79	Navigator Wingman Skin	–
45	Wild Frontier Level Badge	–	80	Wild Frontier Level Badge	–
46	Opening Season Gibraltar Quip	Apex Pack	81	Land of Giants Gibraltar Frame	–
47	50 Apex Coins	–	82	BP Point Boost: +2.5% survival time as BP per squad member	–
48	Gibraltar Tracker—Season 1 Kills	Messenger Octane Skin	83	Apex Pack	–
49	Harvest Peacekeeper Skin	–	84	Patchwork RE-45 Skin	–
50	Wild Frontier Level Badge	–	85	Wild Frontier Level Badge	–
51	Thrill of the Hunt Prowler Skin	–	86	Legendary Apex Pack	–
52	BP Point Boost: +2.5% survival time as BP per squad member	–	87	100 Apex Coins	–
53	Apex Pack	–	88	Slaughterhouse Caustic Frame	–
54	Harvest Devotion Skin	–	89	BP Point Boost: +2.5% survival time as BP per squad member	–
55	Wild Frontier Level Badge	–	90	Wild Frontier Level Badge	–
56	Opening Season Wraith Quip	–	91	Building Bridges Pathfinder Frame	–
57	100 Apex Coins	–	92	BP Point Boost: +2.5% survival time as BP per squad member	–
58	Octane Tracker—Season 1 Kills	–	93	Apex Pack	–
59	Patchwork Mastiff Skin	–	94	Patchwork G7 Scout Skin	–
			95	Wild Frontier Level Badge	–
			96	Open Season Lifeline Quip	–
			97	100 Apex Coins	–
			98	Sharpened Senses Bangalore Frame	–
			99	Harvest R-301 Skin	–

SECRETS & EASTER EGGS

APEX LEGENDS MAY SEEM LIKE A PRETTY STRAIGHTFORWARD GAME AT FIRST GLANCE, BUT THERE'S A LOT GOING ON UNDER THE SURFACE.

NESSIE!

Respawn managed to smuggle a cute Loch Ness Monster Easter egg into the game before the launch of the first season, hiding a secret encounter in the game if you find 10 little Nessie figures . . . and shoot them! Once you've managed to locate all the figures, you can travel to a specific spot on the map and see the creature make an in-game appearance.

TITANFALL REFERENCES

Apex Legends is set 30 years after the events of a previous Respawn game, *Titanfall 2*. But that's not where the connections end. There's also a location in the map called Lastimosa Armory. Anyone who has played *Titanfall 2* will recognize this as a major character's name. Even Nessie made appearances in both previous *Titanfall* games.

HEIRLOOMS

There is a hidden set of items that have a 1% chance of dropping when you open an Apex Pack, known as the *Apex Legends* Heirloom Set. The set features a series of special items for Wraith, including:
• Knife Skin
• Intro Quip
• Banner Pose

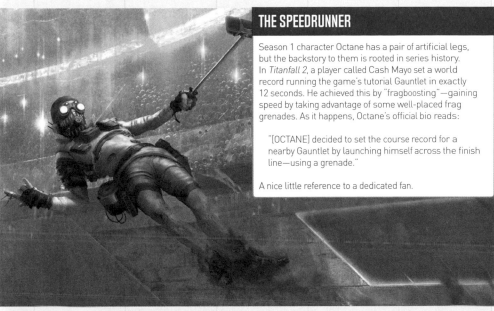

THE SPEEDRUNNER

Season 1 character Octane has a pair of artificial legs, but the backstory to them is rooted in series history. In *Titanfall 2*, a player called Cash Mayo set a world record running the game's tutorial Gauntlet in exactly 12 seconds. He achieved this by "fragboosting"—gaining speed by taking advantage of some well-placed frag grenades. As it happens, Octane's official bio reads:

> "[OCTANE] decided to set the course record for a nearby Gauntlet by launching himself across the finish line—using a grenade."

A nice little reference to a dedicated fan.

A RECURRING CHARACTER?

Bloodhound was not initially designed for *Apex Legends*. The all-seeing scout was originally meant to appear in a *Titanfall* game, according to an almost-complete render included in a *Titanfall* art book. But because the first *Titanfall* launched without a full story mode, it seems a lot of characters were cut.

Now Bloodhound lives—although sadly without the bow and arrow they were originally seen with. What other leftover design ideas and concepts never made it into Respawn's original games? We may never know.

STAY SAFE ONLINE

APEX LEGENDS IS ALL FUN AND GAMES—FOR THE MOST PART. IT'S ALSO AN ONLINE EXPERIENCE WITH OTHER PLAYERS, AND IT PAYS TO REMEMBER THAT.

Apex Legends is a hugely popular game—one that managed to attract a massive 50 million players within its first month online. Not all of those players are going to be as interested as you are in making the game a safe, enjoyable space, so there are a few things you should be aware of.

Though you can turn on voice chat for yourself, there is no way of permanently turning off voice chat for other players—you will have to manually mute them on a game-to-game basis if you want to turn off all incoming chat. Keep that in mind, if you find yourself on a loud team.

After an update early on in the game's life, you can now report players, too. If anything another player says is hateful, inappropriate, upsetting, or threatening, then make sure to use this feature immediately and report that player to Respawn and EA.

DO

Report players. If anything at all makes you feel uncomfortable, you can report players via the end-game screen by pressing the Right Stick.

DO

Know your age rating. In the US, *Apex Legends* is rated 13+, and in the UK/EU it is rated 16+. These aren't legal restrictions, but they are recommended.

DO

Set up parental controls. There will be specific guides to setting up parental controls on Xbox One, PS4, and PC. See online to learn how to do this.

DO

Set your party to Private to prevent random players from joining. This can be done from the Lobby, and helps you stick together with players you know.

DON'T

Be part of the problem. Toxic behavior is prevalent in online gaming: don't make online spaces dangerous or unwelcoming to others.

DON'T

Give out personal information online. Never tell people where you live, give out bank information, or reveal personal knowledge to people you've never met.

DON'T

Spend money without permission. *Apex Legends* is free to download, but does include optional purchases—always get parental consent before buying.

DON'T

Forget to mute players. This can be done in the pre-game screens, or in-game via the menu. You don't have to listen to someone if you don't want to!

PARENTAL CONTROLS

WE'VE ALREADY SHARED SOME TIPS ON STAYING SAFE IN APEX LEGENDS, BUT USING PARENTAL CONTROLS PROVIDES AN ADDED LAYER OF SECURITY.

PLAYSTATION 4

Parents on PS4 consoles can use Parental Settings to enforce content restrictions for their kids, meaning you can control what your children have access to when you're not around to monitor their actions.

To get started, from the PlayStation 4 Home menu simply select [Settings] and then [Parental Controls/Family Management].

Here, most parents may want to consider creating a new Sub Account for their children. This allows the child to have full access to his or her own account (with his or her own username and password), but with restrictions in place that you can choose, which we've outlined below.

CHAT/MESSAGE

When setting up the account, you can opt to block all incoming and outgoing chat and messages. Thanks to the *Apex Legends* Ping system, these features are not vital in-game. Alternatively, your children can choose to talk to their online friends via a mobile or other, more personal, medium.

MONTHLY SPENDING LIMIT

Apex Legends has in-app transactions that can request money from any cards affiliated with the PlayStation account. If you're happy for your child to spend a predetermined amount of money per month in-game, you can establish the limit here. Ensure you set a secure passcode so your child can't change this!

TIME LIMITS

You can limit how much time a child has access to games for each day of the week, or at certain times of day. If you want your child to play less on weekdays and more on weekends, for example, you can set this limit here.

Alternatively, you can set a quota per day or week, too, giving you more control over what your child is doing—and when he or she is doing it.

XBOX ONE

Microsoft prides itself on its robust range of parental controls on the Xbox One, and thanks to the system's integration with Windows, you can even check in and monitor your kids' activities on your PC once you've setup the relevant accounts.

A full breakdown of this easy process can be found online at: support.xbox.com/family

In the meantime, here the four essential options you need to know about when setting up parental controls for Xbox One consoles.

CONTENT RESTRICTIONS

Ensure your children only have access to age-appropriate content by blocking specific apps, games or websites. Restrictions can be customized for each child, that way older kids are not limited to the content set for their younger siblings. Children can request access to games, apps, or websites, which parents can approve or decline. This provides an opportunity for parents and children to talk about appropriate content. Be aware of the *Apex Legends* age rating in your country when adjusting this setting.

PURCHASE CONTROLS

Parents can customize how they permit purchases on Microsoft and Xbox stores through a few different options, and receive an email alert after each purchase. Also, you can add money to your child's account so they can make purchases on their own within a specific limit.

Setting up a Passkey on your Xbox—via a Parent account—will allow you to authorize payments and top-ups to kids accounts.

SCREEN TIME MANAGEMENT

Parents can set screen time limits and schedules for each day of the week. For example, they can limit children to one hour of console time on school days and provide extra time on the weekends.

This option is highly customizable and can be altered by a parent account at any time—so if the day allows for an hour's more screen time one evening but not the other, you can adjust accordingly.

PRIVACY & SAFETY ONLINE

Parents can direct how their children engage and interact with others on Xbox by managing who can communicate and play games with their children, as well as restrict the activity and profile information others can view. In any online game, this is important: you can adjust the settings so that your child can only engage in chat with known accounts (read: friends). Be aware that *Apex Legends* has its own in-game chat which you may want to disable if you don't want your child talking to strangers.

THROW DOWN

GUNS AND ABILITIES AREN'T YOUR ONLY TOOLS IN APEX LEGENDS. THROWABLES CAN BE USED TO DEVASTATING EFFECT, TOO.

There are three types of throwable items in *Apex Legends* at the time of writing, with the promise of more to come. These projectile items can be used to great effect, either defensively or offensively, and can be a crucial tool in your arsenal when the going gets tough. Here's everything you need to know about maximizing the potential of these versatile items. Remember, you can hold only two throwables per inventory slot, so make sure you use them well!

ARC STAR

Once thrown, an Arc Star will stick to any surface (not just on the ground), causing damage on impact and over time. That means you can effectively use these items like sticky grenades. After three seconds, an Arc Star will explode, dealing 70 damage and stunning players for five seconds. Any players caught within the blast radius of the Arc Star will also have their shields disabled.

TIPS

- Stunned enemies will move more slowly and have reduced aim sensitivity. Move in on them while they're vulnerable.

- Disabling shields makes Arc Stars great items for late-game use, when you may be up against Epic- and Legendary-armored enemies.

THERMITE GRENADE

These throwable items explode on impact causing a fiery horizontal line to spread away from the grenade once it lands. Anyone caught in the Thermite Grenade's incendiary barrier will suffer damage over time. Though the horizontal wall that comes from the Thermite Grenade isn't bulletproof, the items can be used to break an enemy's line of sight.

TIPS

- The Thermite Grenade can be used to seal off areas and, as such, is particularly effective in more built-up regions of the map.

- Paired with abilities like Caustic's Nox Gas, these grenades can help rapidly drain otherwise in-cover enemies' health.

FRAG GRENADE

The Frag Grenade is the most classic item in the *Apex Legends* throwables catalogue. It behaves like most grenades from other FPS games. That is to say, the device will explode once thrown after roughly six seconds, and will deal less damage the farther you are from the initial blast. Useful for applying pressure on enemy teams.

TIPS

- Use Frags liberally: there are always more to be found around the map. They're especially useful when it comes to pushing enemies out of cover, or into lines of sight.

- If you're being pursued, don't be afraid to drop a Frag as you run—careless enemies running over them can take serious damage.

BEST LOADOUTS

NOW THAT YOU KNOW WHAT ALL THE WEAPONS IN THE GAME DO, IT'S TIME TO LEARN ABOUT THE BEST COMBINATIONS.

R-301 CARBINE + PEACEKEEPER

Voted by many as the best weapon combo in the game, this setup puts two of the best weapons in *Apex Legends* side by side, and each works well without having to rely on tricky-to-find attachments.

PROS

The weapons are effective at all ranges and can easily down close-range targets without pause.

CONS

They don't provide the best damage for tight firefights, and not a lot of long-range flexibility.

R-301 CARBINE + R-99

Because there is lots of Light Ammo available throughout the map, and these two guns are fairly common spawns, learning to master this setup will generally keep you in the game until those final minutes.

PROS

Use the Carbine for longer-distance engagements and switch to the R-99 when things get personal.

CONS

A combo that is incredibly thirsty for Light Ammo, thanks to the rapid-fire nature of the R-99.

M600 SPITFIRE + WINGMAN

A decent combo that makes up for the Spitfire's tough recoil by relegating its usage to short-range encounters. It burns a lot of Heavy ammo, though, so bear that in mind if you're averse to sniffing it out.

PROS

A weapon pairing that can chew through enemy health at short range, with full-auto support too.

CONS

This combo isn't viable without Extended Heavy Mags and a surplus of Heavy Ammo.

WINGMAN + PEACEKEEPER

A combo that's effective from far away or close-up thanks to the power of each weapon, this setup is the standard Season 1 combo for many players.

PROS

Massively ammo-efficient, so if you don't want to spend your games searching for ammo, this suits you.

CONS

Can be punishing for beginners: no full-auto can hurt if you panic. Attachments highly recommended.

PROWLER + LONGBOW

Using the Prowler to dominate the short and mid-range encounters frees up your Longbow to land high-damage potshots at range. You can swap out the Sniper Rifle for any other Sniper class weapon without too much issue as well.

PROS

You won't need stabilizers with this combo: Prowler doesn't use one and Longbow can do without.

CONS

You'll need an Epic Heavy Extended Mag and a Selectfire Receiver for the Prowler's full-auto mode.

MAKING MOVES

MOBILITY IN APEX LEGENDS—AS IN ALL RESPAWN ENTERTAINMENT TITLES— IS THE NAME OF THE GAME. HERE'S HOW YOU CAN MOVE LIKE A PRO.

Movement is critical to success in *Apex Legends*. We suggest you live by three rules: stay mobile, stay agile, and stay sharp. Stick to this simple mantra and you'll be sure to get the drop on anyone you come up against. Here, we walk you through the tools that *Apex Legends* gives you to run rings around your opponents.

BASIC MOVEMENT

The most straightforward modes of movement in *Apex Legends* may be simple, but it still pays to understand them. Let's break them down:

WALKING

Push on the right analog stick on a console pad to move; use WASD on PC/keyboard. Walking is the default movement in the game.

SPRINTING

Click the right stick on a console pad, or hold LSHIFT on PC to sprint. Sprinting is louder than walking, and will lower your weapons, potentially leaving you vulnerable.

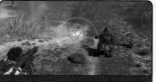

CROUCHING

By default, you can tap the B/Circle button on a console pad to crouch. On PC, you'll need to hold LCTRL, or tap C. Crouching makes you slower, but softens your footsteps.

JUMPING

Jump with the A/X on a console pad, or with SPACE on keyboard. Remember that your jump will always be the same: there's no "charged jump" or anything like that.

SLIDING

Sliding in *Apex Legends* is vital to survival, and you'll often need to slide to keep pace with your allies (and enemies!) in the game. Here are some quick tips about the mechanic:

- Sliding is a handy navigational tool—it's quicker than sprinting for the most part—and is useful defensively too: it makes your character model smaller and more difficult to hit.

- Sliding is triggered by crouching while sprinting. You can slide forward, and you can also "strafe slide," which is handy for avoiding incoming fire.

- Don't just slide on hills. Sliding on flat surfaces also works, though it won't take you as far. You can also slide uphill—but not far. Experiment with sliding, sprinting, and moving to find your ideal rhythm.

- If you have too much vertical momentum, you won't be able to slide. Also, your velocity will cap at a certain speed, so you won't continue to accelerate down a hill consistently.

CLIMBING

Climbing is necessary to reach higher ground and reposition yourself in the game. The whole King's Canyon map was made with this feature in mind, so make sure to put it to good use!

- You can almost always climb higher than you think! Run up a wall, look up, and push—you'd be surprised at how far you can go!

- If you see it, you can climb it—never forget that. Practically everything on the map is climbable, and you can use that to your advantage when stalking your enemies.

- There's no fall damage in *Apex Legends*. Climb, fall, and repeat. You learn by making mistakes.

- Zip lines work both ways, and are an excellent means of climbing as well as descending.

The quickest way to move in the game is by "slide jumping": holster your weapon, sprint into a slide, then at the peak of your momentum, jump. Hit the ground running, sprint into a slide for a second, then slide and repeat!

THE RING

THE RING IS THE FORCE THAT DRIVES EVERY GAME OF APEX LEGENDS, PUSHING YOU CLOSER AND CLOSER TO VICTORY... OR DEFEAT.

Apex Legends may differ from the Battle Royale genre in many ways, but it still uses some of the classic tropes—the Ring being one of them. The Ring (known as the Storm in *Fortnite* or the Playzone in *PUBG*) determines where you can play, and shrinks the playable map over time. If you want to know how small the Ring can get, and its rough size per stage, you can refer to the handy guide on the opposite page. If you're wondering what you need to do and how you need to deal with the Ring as it bears down on you, then you're in luck: we've assembled a list of tips for you here as well. The Ring may seem like an unstoppable force determined to kill you... but used intelligently, it can be another tool in your arsenal.

DO

Keep the timer in mind. It's there for a reason: don't be caught short and have to outrun the Ring as it shrinks.

DO

Know your limits. If you're hungry for loot, but know your healing items won't stave off the next Ring's damage, don't get greedy.

DO

Learn the Wait/Closing rhythm. As the rounds start to shorten, get ahead of the game and into cover to get the drop on your enemies.

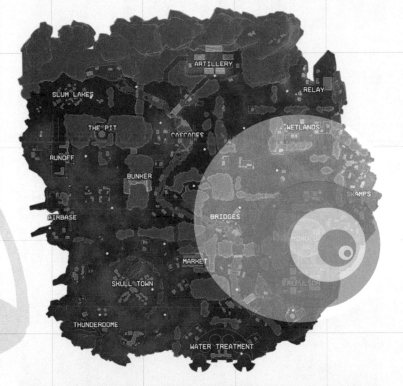

DON'T

Be scared of the first few Ring closes. The first stage only does one damage per tick to you, meaning you can easily outlive it and create ambushes on unsuspecting enemies.

DON'T

Be hemmed in. After Round 5, the Ring caps at 10 damage per tick. Quick journeys in and out of the Ring to flank enemies may be worth it!

DON'T

Forget to check your perimeter. You're never safe in Apex Legends, and treating the Ring like a wall will just make that clearer than ever.

ROUND	WAIT PERIOD	LOSING PERIOD	DAMAGE PER TICK	RING DIAMETER	% AREA OF PREVIOUS RING
1	4m	2m30s	1	115m	26% (of map area)
2	3m30s	1m3s	2	680m	37%
3	3m	35s	5	410m	36%
4	2m15s	28s	5	105m	6.6%
5	2m	18s	10	80m	58%
6	1m30s	5s	10	40m	25%
7	2m	6.5s	10	4m	1%
8	20s	1s	10	0m	0%

SKIN IN THE GAME

THE WHOLE POINT OF PLAYING APEX LEGENDS AND UNLOCKING MORE PACKS IS TO GET BETTER SKINS, RIGHT? HERE'S WHAT YOU SHOULD BE AIMING FOR.

THE BEST LEGEND SKINS

BANGALORE

THE SPACEWALKER
Clean colors, sharp shoulder pads, and space-age tech make this one of Bangalore's coolest skins.

BLOODHOUND

IMPERIAL WARRIOR
Inspired by Old Earth's most ferocious Japanese warriors, this skin is perfect for a feud.

CAUSTIC

SIXTH SENSE
Is it strange that a man whose passive ability lets him see through smoke blinds himself? Hmm.

GIBRALTAR

DARK SIDE
The most intimidating player in the Apex Games gets even more scary with this imposing face paint.

LIFELINE

LONDON CALLING
Lifeline shows off her punk inspirations in a throwback to one of Old Earth's most notable fashions.

MIRAGE

THE AVENGER
Full-body armor plates—all in stylish yellow—make Mirage seem more Tony Stark than anything else.

PATHFINDER

ANGEL CITY PACER
Named after a map that debuted in Titanfall, this skin makes Pathfinder look like an F1 car.

OCTANE

EL DIABLO
With a mask that makes him look like a Japanese oni, this skin brings new meaning to "terrifying speed."

WRAITH

THE LIBERATOR
This is the look Wraith had when she woke up, angry and alone, in an underground science facility.

THE BEST WEAPON SKINS

ASSAULT RIFLES

FLATLINE
The Spine Chiller

HEMLOCK
The Glorious One

R-301
Dynastic Cycle

HAVOC
Quantum Chaos

SMGs

ALTERNATOR
Search & Rescue

PROWLER
The Dark Realm

R-99
The Alchemist

LMGs

DEVOTION
Nitro Kustom

M600 SPITFIRE
Flying Warhawk

SNIPERS

LONGBOW
Big Game Hunter

G7 SCOUT
The Golden Dragon

KRABER
The Life Saver

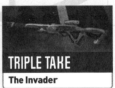
TRIPLE TAKE
The Invader

SHOTGUNS

EVA-8
The Firebreather

MASTIFF
Warp Zone

MOZAMBIQUE
Brother of the Blade

PEACEKEEPER
The Superstar

PISTOLS

RE-45
The Pride

P2020
Green Mamba

WINGMAN
Merciless Wing

STATS, FACTS & FIGURES

APEX LEGENDS HAS BROKEN RECORD AFTER RECORD SINCE ITS LAUNCH. HERE ARE JUST A FEW OF THE GAME'S ASTONISHING NUMBERS.

THE RACE TO 10 MILLION

Respawn and EA celebrated a massive 10 million players pretty early on in the game's life—but how does that compare to its genre rival, *Fortnite*?

Well, by all accounts, it seems it took *Fortnite two weeks* to reach the 10 million figure... and it took *Apex Legends only three days*!

50 MILLION AND COUNTING!

At the time of writing, *Apex Legends* has over 50,000,000 players. That's roughly the same amount of players that *Pokémon Go* had when it launched way back in 2016. And you can expect that number to grow in the not-too-distant future!

FINISH HIM

Finishers are lengthy, leave you exposed, and are difficult to use in the midst of an intense firefight... but that hasn't stopped millions of players from wheeling them out to take out enemies in style.

A month after being released, over 158 million finishers had been used in *Apex Legends*!

158 M FINISHERS USED

ULTIMATUM

Ultimates are used often in the game—they charge up quickly and can be used to lay down some real damage or escape tight situations. Still, that doesn't soften the blow of knowing there were over 1,203,000,000 ultimates used in the game's first 30 days online! That's 1.23 billion! That's a lot of zeros.

APEX LEGENDS IN NUMBERS

Apex Legends enjoyed unprecedented success in its first month. Here are just a few more astonishing figures.

31 BILLION
Pings placed

170 MILLION
Respawns

16.5 MILLION
Death box Graveyards made

ACHIEVEMENT CHECKLIST

IF YOU NEED A LITTLE EXTRA INCENTIVE TO KEEP YOU PLAYING AND LEVELING UP IN APEX LEGENDS, THERE ARE PLENTY OF ACHIEVEMENTS YOU CAN CHASE.

☐ **The Player – 100G / Silver**
Description: Reach player level 50.
Tips: Just keep playing!

☐ **Decked Out – 75G / Bronze**
Description: Equip a legendary Helmet and Body Armor at the same time.
Tips: Play with friends who are happy to drop items, let you equip, and give back.

☐ **Team Player – 75G / Bronze**
Description: Respawn a teammate.
Tips: Be attentive, always know where your nearest Respawn Point is, make sure to grab allies' Banners when possible.

☐ **Fully Kitted – 75G / Bronze**
Description: Equip a fully kitted weapon.
Tips: Equip a Legendary attachment in every slot of a weapon. Pistols are the easiest for this—they only have two slots.

☐ **Jumpmaster – 75G / Bronze**
Description: Be the jumpmaster 5 times.
Tips: Just keep playing, and don't relinquish control, even if you're feeling pressured!

☐ **Well-Rounded – 100G / Silver**
Description: Deal 5,000 damage with 8 different Legends.
Tips: Keep playing, and don't get too attached to any one hero. Make sure to rotate frequently.

☐ **Kill Leader – 75G / Bronze**
Description: Become the Kill Leader.
Tips: Try and capitalize on under-equipped enemies early in the game if you luck out with a good gun.

☐ **Apex Offense – 75G / Bronze**
Description: Win the game as an offensive character.
Tips: See Wraith, Bangalore, Octane, and Mirage character pages.

☐ **Apex Defense – 75G / Bronze**
Description: Win the game as a defensive character.
Tips: See Gibraltar and Caustic character pages.

☐ **Apex Support – 75G / Bronze**
Description: Win the game as a support character.
Tips: See Pathfinder and Lifeline character pages.

☐ **Apex Recon – 75G / Bronze**
Description: Win the game as a recon character.
Tips: See Bloodhound character page.

☐ **Apex Legend – 125G / Gold**
Description: Win a game with 8 different Legends.
Tips: Keep playing, keep getting better, keep learning new tricks, and keep mastering the systems and you'll get this eventually.